THE ESSENTIAL
BAROQUE
COLLECTION
FOR SOLO PIANO

CHESTER MUSIC
part of The Music Sales Group

London / New York / Paris / Sydney / Copenhagen / Berlin / Madrid / Tokyo

Published by
Chester Music Limited,
14/15 Berners Street, London, W1T 3LJ, England.

Exclusive distributors:
Music Sales Corporation,
257 Park Avenue South,
New York, New York 10010 USA.

Music Sales Limited,
Distribution Centre, Newmarket Road, Bury St Edmunds,
Suffolk, IP33 3YB, England.

Music Sales Pty Limited,
120 Rothschild Avenue, Rosebery,
NSW 2018, Australia.

Order No. CH70576
ISBN 1-84609-225-6
This book © Copyright 2006 by Chester Music Limited.

Arranging and engraving supplied by Camden Music.

Printed in the United States of America.

www.musicsales.com

Your Guarantee of Quality:
As publishers, we strive to produce every book
to the highest commercial standards.

The music has been freshly engraved. Particular care has been
given to specifying acid-free, neutral-sized paper made from pulps
which have not been elemental chlorine bleached.

This pulp is from farmed sustainable forests
and was produced with special regard for the environment.

Throughout, the printing and binding have been planned to ensure a sturdy,
attractive publication which should give years of enjoyment.

If your copy fails to meet our high standards, please inform us
and we will gladly replace it.

THE BAROQUE PERIOD

The word 'baroque' was originally used as a derogatory term (the original Portuguese word *barroco* means a misshapen pearl) to describe music that is excessively complicated and inelegant. For the generation after J.S. Bach, there were many who regarded the earlier style with distaste. Jean-Jacques Rousseau, for example, described baroque music as 'confused, charged with modulations and dissonances, the melody is harsh and unnatural, the intonation awkward, the movement constrained'. Not until the 20th century was the term 'baroque' used without its negative associations.

The baroque era was a long one, ranging roughly from 1600 to 1750. It initially emerged out of the renaissance as Italian composers like Monteverdi began to move away from the traditional smooth, vocal counterpoint of the previous era in order to explore contrasts of various kinds and to exploit increasingly theatrical devices in their works. The new genre of opera began to flourish (Monteverdi's *Orfeo* received its first performance in 1607). Composers became fascinated by the contrasts between different dynamics, different speeds, different types of texture, and even spatial contrasts (the Venetian composer Giovanni Gabrielli for example, composed music where different choirs sang to each other from different parts of a church building).

Perhaps the most significant development of all was the way in which baroque composers began to re-think the make-up of music itself. In renaissance music, the bass voice is treated in a similar melodic manner to all the other voices. During the baroque period, this changed drastically as the bass line became the dominant element. Now, the bass line dictated the harmony that went above it and bass lines began to move in a more assertive manner as composers began to enjoy travelling from key to key. The use of stronger bass lines meant that composers could give their music a clearer sense of direction and structure than ever before. This in turn gave rise to a huge repertoire of new instrumental music (before the baroque era, the majority of composed music was vocal. Instruments, if employed at all, tended merely to play along with vocal lines). In a sense, we owe our modern understanding of the way music functions to these innovations. The very idea of 'melody with bass line' is an invention of the baroque period. So too is the idea of a song with accompaniment. Instrumental music—either solo or accompanied by a keyboard instrument—became increasingly popular, especially in the fashionable new form of the sonata.

The new significance of the bass-line led baroque composers to delight in structures that exploited the bass-line such as the chaconne (or ground bass) in which continuous repetition of the bass line underpins the composition. Many pieces of great technical skill and beauty such as Purcell's *When I am Laid in Earth* or Pachelbel's *Canon* are constructed in this way. Another key development of the baroque era is that of the concerto with its dramatic contrasts of instrumental texture and its theatrical dialogue between soloist and ensemble. When the Italian violinist-composer, Arcangelo Corelli's concertos were published in 1714 they created a sensation across Europe with their colourful instrumental effects.

In the following generation another Italian, Antonio Vivaldi, led the way in discovering new and exciting innovations in concerto writing. Many of his concertos, including *The Four Seasons*, contain descriptive elements and have poetic titles. Vivaldi (a famous violinist in his own life-time) explored new avenues of instrumental virtuosity in many of his compositions. His concertos were the first to use the standard three-movement (fast-slow-fast) structure and his pioneering use of assertive rhythmic themes influenced younger contemporaries like Bach and Handel.

The baroque era came to a remarkable climax in the first half of the 18th century as a generation of brilliant young composers began to find ever-richer possibilities with the mature style. In Italy, Domenico Scarlatti composed a dazzling sequence of keyboard sonatas, breathtaking in their range of emotion and technique. The young Pergolesi (who died at the age of 26) managed to bequeath to the world of music a number of important pieces (especially his *Stabat Mater*) strikingly original in their melodic beauty and emotional directness. In Germany, Telemann (a far more popular composer in his lifetime than Bach) was the most prolific composer in history.

However it is in the work of Bach and Handel (both born within days of each other in neighbouring towns) that baroque music achieved its summit in very different ways. Handel, a cosmopolitan figure, learnt his craft in Germany and Italy where he established a reputation for compositional brilliance before travelling to London, where he lived for the rest of his life, writing the greatest Italian operas of the age, inventing the English oratorio and composing a magnificent array of concertos and other concert works.

Bach, on the other hand, remained a provincial composer in northern Germany all his life, working within the protestant tradition and producing a range of works that were richer in technique and expressive power than any other composer of his time. His contrapuntal mastery, combined with an infallible feeling for harmony and all the ingredients of baroque music listed above, have ensured him a pre-eminent place, not only in the music of his own time but in the history of western music.

However, the younger generation (most notably Bach's son, Carl Philipp Emmanuel Bach) rejected the titanic achievements of the high-baroque era which they saw as unnecessarily complicated, and began to forge a simpler, more direct style which led the way to the birth of classicism, but that is another story…

BAROQUE COMPOSERS

Carl Philipp Emanuel Bach (1714–1788) was the second son of J.S. Bach and, during his lifetime, was the most famous member of the illustrious family. In his later years he was known as 'the great Bach' and revered by Haydn and Mozart (who once said of him 'he is the father of us all'.)

C.P.E. Bach worked in Berlin as harpsichordist to Frederick the Great. He remained in the king's service for 28 difficult years before eventually obtaining his permission to move to Hamburg where he became the town music director (an enormous job, previously done by Telemann). C.P.E. Bach's vast output of keyboard music, concertos, sinfonias and religious works had a major influence on the emerging classical style.

Johann Sebastian Bach (1685–1750) was the greatest musical genius of the baroque period and some would argue the most important composer in history. His working life was spent in provincial Germany. For the last 27 years he was a music director in Leipzig.

Bach excelled in every genre: his incomparable output of keyboard music (always composed in the most systematic manner—e.g. his 48 Preludes and Fugues in every key) forms a central place in his output. His concertos—especially the set known as the Brandenburg—outstrip their models (particularly Vivaldi) in terms of quality and depth of invention. His peerless religious music includes more than 200 cantatas as well as the sublime *St Matthew* and *St John Passions*.

Bach was the greatest organist of his age and, by the time of his death, was widely esteemed in Germany for the 'learned' quality of his music. It was not until the Bach revival of the 19th Century (led by the 18-year-old Mendelssohn) that Bach's true greatness began to be appreciated worldwide.

Arcangelo Corelli (1653–1713) was universally regarded as the finest violinist of his age. During his lifetime he published five sets of sonatas which rapidly gained eminent status in baroque musical circles. His set of concerti grossi Op. 6 (including the famous Christmas Concerto) were published, after his death, in 1714 and became instant classics across Europe. Corelli was considered to be the composer to emulate and his work became a kind of 'gold standard' of compositional excellence for years to come.

John Dowland (1563–1626) was most famous in his lifetime for his expressive lute playing. He performed to Queen Elizabeth I in 1592 but was deeply disappointed thereafter not to receive a court position. He decided to travel, first to Italy, then Germany and finally to Denmark where he was appointed lutenist to Charles IV. Finally, in 1612, he returned to London as court lutenist to James I.

Dowland was a composer of genius, specialising in songs and short works for lute and string consort. His works are famously melancholic with titles like *In Darknesse let me dwell* and *Lachrime, or seaven Teares*. The latter is a superb collection of pavans and galliards for string consort.

Orlando Gibbons (1583–1625) was an exceptionally versatile English composer, highly regarded in his own lifetime for his accomplishment as a keyboard player. Gibbons was a master of vocal writing. His madrigals are among the finest of their period and his anthem *O Clap Your Hands Together* is a model of expression and shape. Gibbons also composed a number of important keyboard works.

George Frideric Handel (1685–1759) was born the same year as J.S. Bach, a composer with whom he shares pre-eminent status in the baroque period. Unlike Bach, he was internationally celebrated during his lifetime.

Handel first won fame in Italy where he developed his extraordinary facility as an opera composer. On arriving in London in 1710, Handel's operas soon became a sensation and the young composer attracted a number of important aristocratic patrons. When his old employer, George of Hanover, became king in 1714, Handel composed his *Water Music* for a royal serenade on the Thames.

Handel ran his own opera company (for which he composed a continuous stream of operas) until the 1730s when Italian opera became less fashionable. Undaunted, Handel went on to write oratorios instead, performing his own organ concertos as interval entertainment. To this late period belong his masterpieces, *Esther, Saul, Xerxes, Semele* and *Messiah*. His magisterial anthem *Zadok the Priest* was written for the coronation of George II in 1727.

Johann Pachelbel (1653–1706) was a leading German organist and composer who lived a somewhat restless life, taking up various church posts throughout his career, but ending up where he started in Nuremburg. For a period he was friendly with Bach's father and his organ music influenced Johann Sebastian. Pachelbel composed a considerable amount of fine church music including 13 settings of the Magnificat. His famous Canon is written over a ground bass (or repeating bass line).

Giovanni Battista Pergolesi (1710–1736) was born near Ancona, in Italy. He was the only surviving son of a surveyor and suffered throughout his life from tuberculosis.

He was a composer of unusual gifts whose work failed to achieve success during his short life. He worked in Naples for a while, composing operas and sacred pieces. In 1734 he moved to Rome but his health began to deteriorate. His famous *Stabat Mater* was written while convalescing in a Franciscan Monastery.

Pergolesi was probably the youngest great composer in history. His death, at the age of 26, robbed the world of a major talent. Ironically, in the years following his death, his compositions achieved enormous posthumous fame.

Henry Purcell (1659–1695) was a child prodigy. Whilst an eight-year-old chorister in the Chapel Royal, he was already composing songs. He was employed as 'composer for the violins' in Westminster Abbey at the age of 17 and became organist there two years later. His early anthems and viol consorts demonstrate unusual emotional depth and a complete mastery of their genres.

Throughout the 1680s Purcell devoted his energies to church music and, as his fame increased, he turned to Royal odes and theatrical works, collaborating with John Dryden and other leading playwrights. His most famous opera *Dido and Aeneas* was composed for a girls' school in Chelsea in 1689.

Purcell's magnificent funeral music for Queen Mary in 1694 precipitated his own death the following year. Like Mozart and Schubert, his early death was a musical tragedy.

Domenico Scarlatti (1685–1757). Born the same year as Bach and Handel, Scarlatti struggled hard to gain independence from the influence of his famous father, Alessandro Scarlatti (eventually Domenico took legal action against his father in 1717). Around this time, his legendary talents as a keyboard player led to a keyboard contest with Handel.

Scarlatti took various court posts around Europe before settling finally in Madrid where he enjoyed the special patronage of the musical *Infanta Maria Barbara*. He was made a Knight of the Order of Santiago in 1738.

Scarlatti's reputation rests on his superb collection of 500 keyboard sonatas which explore a dazzling array of styles, exotic harmonies and keyboard techniques (sometimes imitating the Spanish guitar). Like Chopin and Liszt a century later, he was the most colourful keyboard composer of his era.

Jan Sweelinck (1562–1621) was the leading organist in Holland at the end of the renaissance. He was famous for his brilliant and imaginative improvisations, and was much in demand as a consultant, testing new organs in Dutch cities.

Sweelinck was a superb keyboard composer. His numerous organ works include fantasias, toccatas and sets of variations. He also wrote a number of madrigals and other vocal compositions.

George Philipp Telemann (1681–1767) was a composer of extraordinary energy and productivity. By the age of ten he had mastered several instruments (including violin, flute, harpsichord and zither) but his mother wanted him to study law. Consequently, he enrolled at the University of Leipzig but abandoned his studies for an active musical career in the city.

In 1721 Telemann moved to the coveted post of music director in Hamburg. His schedule was gruelling: endless church music had to be written, concerts organised and incidental music provided for all occasions. In 1722 he became director of the Hamburg Opera for which he wrote 12 works. During this period he built a considerable reputation (he was much more famous than his friend J.S. Bach). Telemann was a pioneer of the *gallant* style, and his finely crafted music paved the way for the early classical style.

Antonio Vivaldi (1678–1741) was a colourful figure. Born in Venice, he became a priest in 1704 and subsequently taught violin in a girls' orphanage in Venice. There he established an excellent touring orchestra for whom he wrote many of his concertos. He also composed numerous operas and religious works but it was primarily as a violin virtuoso that he became famous throughout Europe. In 1737 his love affair with a singer got him into trouble with the papal authorities who banned performances of his operas in Italy.

Vivaldi pioneered a lively new concerto style that was to influence Bach and Handel. After his death, Vivaldi's work was neglected until the 20th century. Today he is one of the most popular baroque composers.

Domenico Zipoli (1688–1726) was born in Tuscany. He was an accomplished harpsichordist and studied briefly with Scarlatti. In 1716, he became a Jesuit and travelled to Seville. The following year, he took the radical step of emigrating to Paraguay where he studied theology in preparation for ordination as a priest. Sadly, he died of tuberculosis before the bishop arrived for his ordination ceremony. Zipoli composed a mass in Paraguay as well other religious works and keyboard pieces.

Solfeggietto

Composed by Carl Philipp Emanuel Bach

9

Sheep May Safely Graze

Composed by Johann Sebastian Bach

to Coda

12

D.C. al Coda ⊕

⊕ Coda

rall.

13

Air On The G String

(from Suite in D)

Composed by Johann Sebastian Bach

Badinerie

(from Suite No. 2 in B minor)

Composed by Johann Sebastian Bach

Brandenburg Concerto No.3 in G
(1st movement)

Composed by Johann Sebastian Bach

19

Harpsichord Concerto No.5 in F minor

(1st movement)

Composed by Johann Sebastian Bach

Toccata and Fugue in D minor

Composed by Johann Sebastian Bach

Prestissimo (♩ = 160)

Maestoso (♩ = 96)

rall.

allarg. molto

Two-part Invention No.8 in F major

Composed by Johann Sebastian Bach

Sleepers, Wake!

Composed by Johann Sebastian Bach

Prelude in C

Composed by Johann Sebastian Bach

Christmas Concerto
(2nd movement)

Composed by Arcangelo Corelli

Arranged by Jerry Lanning

Christmas Concerto
(3rd movement 'Pastorale')

Composed by Arcangelo Corelli

Arranged by Jerry Lanning

Largo (♩. = 52)

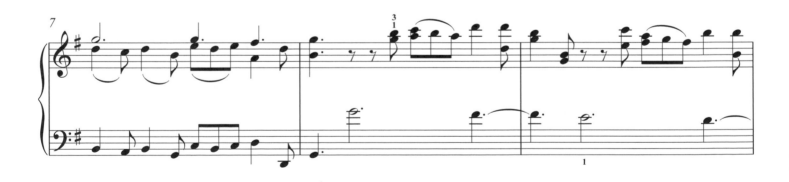

Lachrimae Antiquae
(Flow My Tears)

Composed by John Dowland

Queen Elizabeth Her Galliard

Composed by John Dowland

Arranged by Jerry Lanning

Moderato (♩ = 84)

O Clap Your Hands

Composed by Orlando Gibbons

Arranged by Andrew Skirrow

Moderate

The Arrival of the Queen of Sheba

(from 'Solomon')

Composed by George Frideric Handel

Largo: Ombra Mai Fu

(from 'Xerxes')

Composed by George Frideric Handel

The Harmonious Blacksmith

Composed by George Frideric Handel

68

Lascia Ch'io Pianga
(from 'Rinaldo')

Composed by George Frideric Handel

Overture
(Sinfony from 'Messiah')

Composed by George Frideric Handel
Arranged by Jerry Lanning

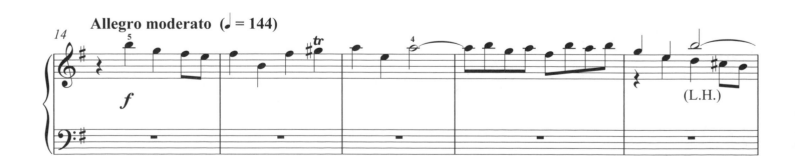

Sarabande in D minor

Composed by George Frideric Handel

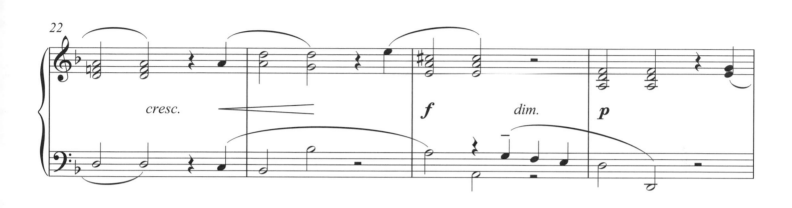

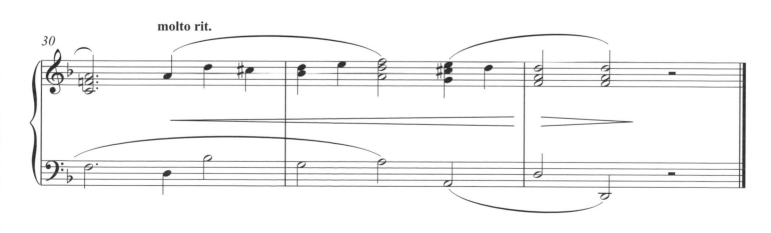

See The Conqu'ring Hero Come

(from 'Judas Maccabaeus')

Composed by George Frideric Handel

p (mp 2nd time)

Water Music: Allegro
(from the Suite in D major)

Composed by George Frideric Handel

Arranged by Jerry Lanning

Allegro (♩ = 120)

Water Music: Hornpipe

(from the Suite in D major)

Composed by George Frideric Handel

Water Music: Overture
(from the Suite in F major)

Composed by George Frideric Handel
Arranged by Jerry Lanning

Water Music: Allegro
(from the Suite in F major)

Composed by George Frideric Handel

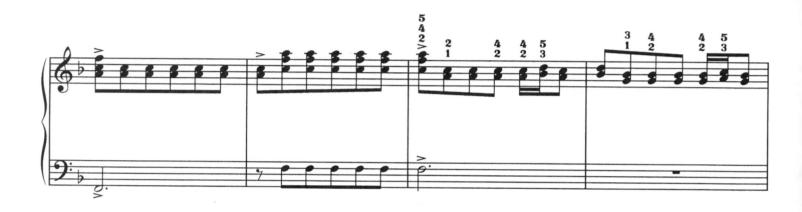

Water Music: Air
(from the Suite in F major)

Composed by George Frideric Handel

Water Music: Presto
(from the Suite in F major)

Composed by George Frideric Handel

Arranged by Jerry Lanning

Da Capo

Zadok The Priest

Composed by George Frideric Handel

Andante maestoso

Canon in D

Composed by Johann Pachelbel

Gigue

Composed by Johann Pachelbel

Arranged by Jerry Lanning

Stabat Mater

Composed by Giovanni Battista Pergolesi

When I Am Laid In Earth

(from 'Dido and Aeneas')

Composed by Henry Purcell

Suite No.4 in A minor

Composed by Henry Purcell

CORANT. Maestoso

SARABAND. Adagio

Thou Knowest, Lord
(Funeral Music for Queen Mary)

Composed by Henry Purcell

Sonata in G major

Composed by Alessandro Scarlatti

Arioso

Composed by Alessandro Scarlatti

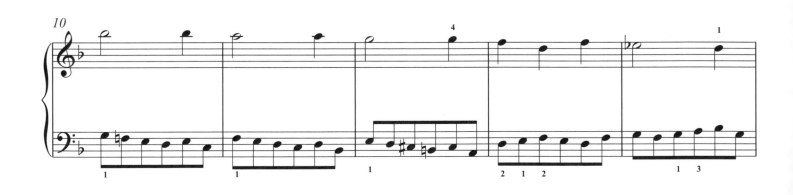

Toccata

Composed by Jan Pieterszoon Sweelinck

Allegro moderato

Spring (1st Movement)
(from 'The Four Seasons' Op.8, No.1-4)

Composed by Antonio Vivaldi
Arranged by Barry Todd

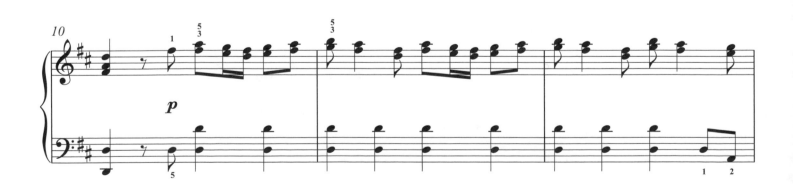

Summer (2nd Movement)

(from 'The Four Seasons' Op.8, No.1-4)

Composed by Antonio Vivaldi

Arranged by Barry Todd

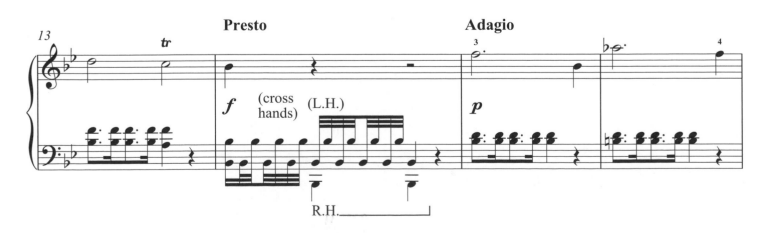

Autumn (1st Movement)

(from 'The Four Seasons' Op.8, No.1-4)

Composed by Antonio Vivaldi
Arranged by Barry Todd

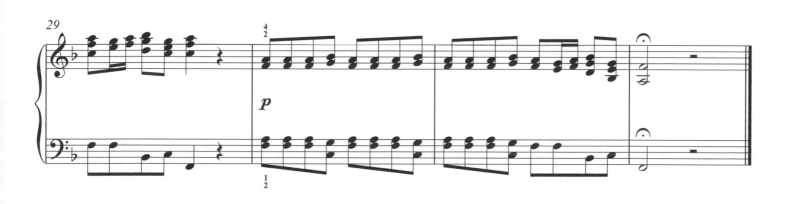

Winter (3rd Movement)
(from 'The Four Seasons' Op.8, No.1-4)

Composed by Antonio Vivaldi

Arranged by Barry Todd

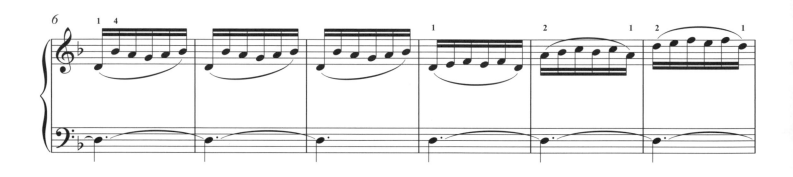

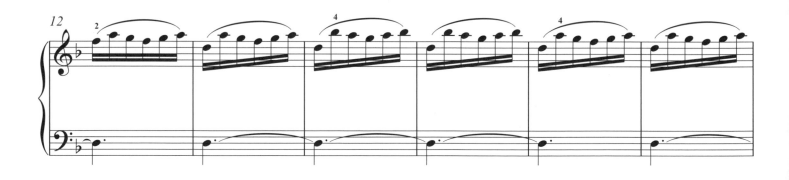

Beatus Vir
(from Gloria)

Composed by Antonio Vivaldi

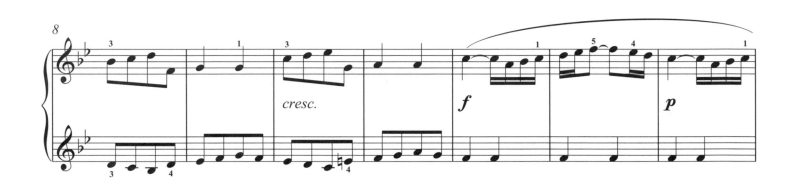

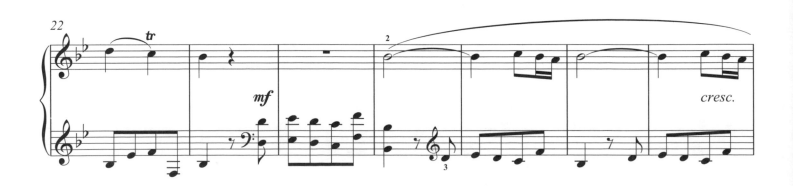

Concerto No.2, 1st movement

(from 'L'Estro Armonico')

Composed by Antonio Vivaldi

143

Gloria

Composed by Antonio Vivaldi
Arranged by Quentin Thomas

senza rall.

149

Un Certo Non So Che

Composed by Antonio Vivaldi
Arranged by Quentin Thomas

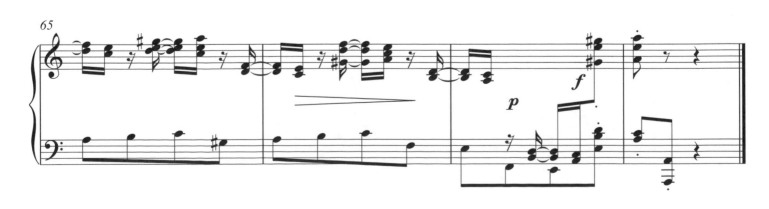

Theme And Variations
(from Partita In A Minor)

Composed by Domenico Zipoli

Moderato

Variation 1

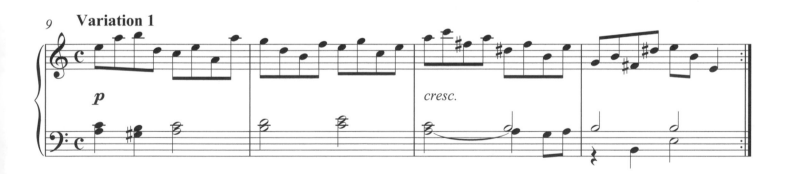

Variation 6. Allegro

Variation 7. Molto vivace

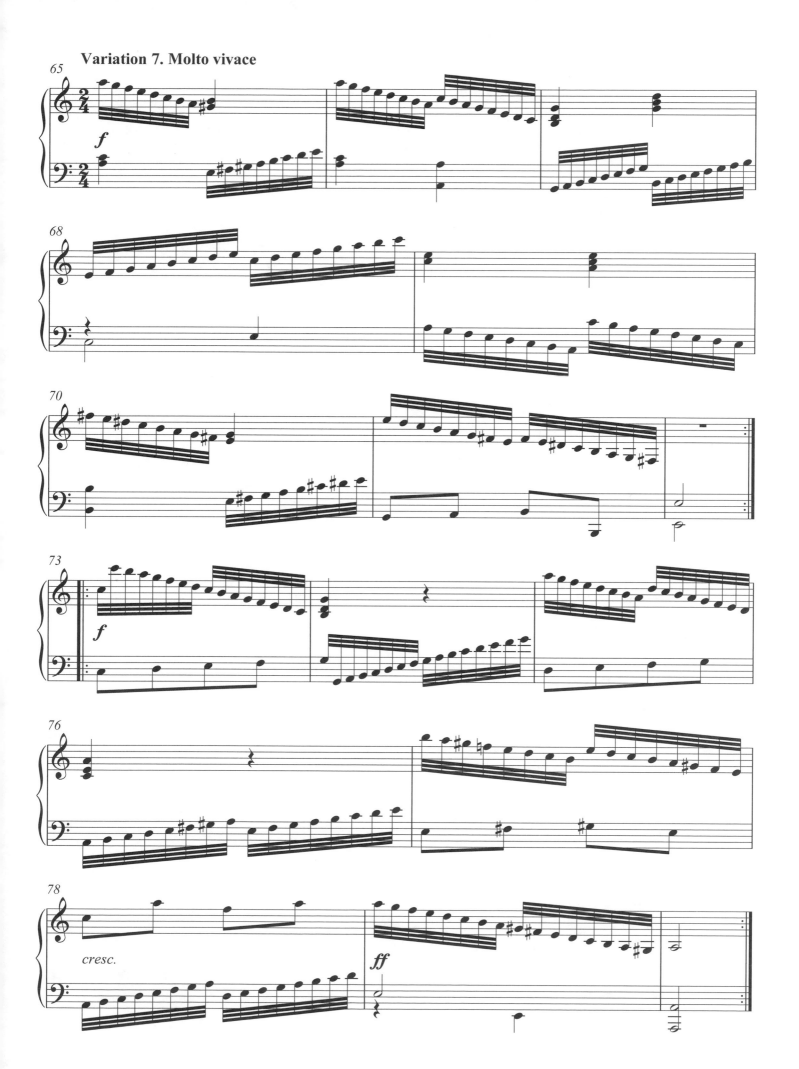

157

Fantasia in B minor

Composed by Georg Philipp Telemann

159

123456789